LIFE'S CHOICES
CAN MAKE YOU OR BREAK YOU

How you end up in life
Depends on choices you make
The friends you choose,
The job you choose
The partner you choose.
Choices   affect   your life.

Life is all about choices
Actions not theories and voices
 good choices make   life a bliss
Bad choices make   life an abyss

Ultimately people are responsible for their own
choices, reaping the rewards or paying the
consequences of those choices!

BY   S. ELIA

LIFE'S CHOICES

People come and people go
That's life on the go
If it's your time to come, you will come
If it's your time to go, you will go
 no choice when you come
No choice when you go
That's life on the go

People come and people go
No choice when you come
No choice when you go

What counts is how you live
What status you achieve
 the quality of life you live

But in the time in between
What counts is what is within
When you come and when you go
What matters is the choices you make
Good choices will make you
Bad choices will break you

Life is all about choice
good choices will make your life full
Bad choice will make your life bad
How to live a life full or a life empty
Life keeps coming , life keeps going
Waiting for nobody TO RE DO a choice

There is time you come
There is time to go
Nobody knows when its time to come
Nobody knows when is time to go
Some   will live long
 Some will live short
But always on the go

If you like to flirt
Chasing after every skirt
You end up with the dirt

No place to hung your   shirt
If your choice is doing drugs
You might   end up in a bag

Life is all about choices
Actions not theories and voices
Good choices gives   joy
Bad choices gives annoy
 good choice makes   life a bliss
Bad choice makes   life an abyss

How you end up in life
Depends on choices you make
The friends you choose,
The job you choose
The partner you choose.
Choices   affect   your life.

People come and go all the time. All people come in this world naked and nothing else. Not even a coat to protect them   from the elements of the weather. Some will live long and others will live short. Some will be rich and some will be poor and life is unpredictable. It all depends on the choices people make.

Here is the story of Peter Williams and the choices he made in his life.
 Peter Williams was born in affluent family. He was the only child in his family. His parents were ecstatic when peter was born. both parents were in their early forties when they got married and settle in their city.

They were both professional   People. his mother Janet was working for the government and his father john was a charter accountant working in a good accounting company. They were making good salaries and they had a comfortable living. They had their own home and they both had their own automobile.

They were both busy with their professions but they wanted to have kids and a family.   Three years to the day they were married Janet Williams happily announced that she was pregnant.

John Williams was walking on cloud nine when he heard the news. He told his wife that he was very happy for the good news and treated his wife to a nice dinner in the nearby restaurant.

The following nine months they were very happy and they anxiously were waiting for the time when their child will finally arrive and make the dream of their lives a reality. They prepared and decorated the baby's room with nice baby furniture and everything else needed for the baby's room.

It was a sunny Saturday morning when Janet's water broke and it was time for a short trip to the hospital for the delivery of her baby. John drove his wife to the hospital where Janet's doctor and his team were waiting for her to deliver her baby.

Six hours after arriving in hospital Janet gave birth to a beautiful healthy baby boy with a head full of hair and bright blue eyes.

John   and Janet were   ecstatic full of happiness and joy. He hugged his wife and he even hugged the whole team that delivered his baby boy , the doctor and the nurses.

Two days later Janet was released from the

hospital and went home .
Janet was tired from the delivery of her baby but
happy that she was finally home with her husband
and her new baby.
 John took two weeks off work to be with his
wife and son and helping out   any help they
needed. Janet   was recovering nicely and she was
nursing her baby .
They name their baby boy , Peter , the same name
that johns father had.
  John's father was very happy that he finally had a
grandson named after him and he declared happily
that he was going to pay all the tuitions necessary

for his grandson's education. John and Janet thank both the grandfather Peter and grandmother Annette for their generous offer.

Janet had a maternity leave for a full year from her work with the government and she stayed home looking after   baby Peter.
Baby peter was growing day by day and before you know it he was one year old. John and Janet had a big birthday party for him and they invited other kids and his grandfather peter and grandmother Annette . That was a wonderful and memorable birthday party with the birthday boy blowing off the one candle on his birthday cake and enjoying eating some of the cake. All the kids sang the happy birthday songs for little peter.

Janet went back to her work and she had to hire a live in nanny to take care of little Peter. The nanny was a very caring girl and she loved taking

care of little peter.   She was taking him for a walk in the near by park and little peter had a good time playing with the park's amenities. Little peter was growing up fast and he was the joy and the happiness of his parents and grandparents. Grandpa Peter was   so happy to spend time with little peter taking him to the neighborhood parks and buying him his favorite ice-cream.

Little peter was growing up fast and soon it was time to go to kindergarten . Peter liked the kindergarten and met many new friends there. His best friend there was Roy who lived closed to the school with his family. Roy and peter spend long hours playing together and they often visited each others homes. Their parents became close friends

too and had  Dinners and
entertainment in their homes.
Peter and Roy after kindergarten went to the same
public school and they were always in the same
class . They were both very smart kids and they
always got good marks and impressive reports for
their school work.
Peter always enjoyed   the company of his
grandparents and especially his grandpa peter.
They often had long walks in the near park where
he played and the local ice-cream parlor . Peter
loved his vanilla ice-cream.
When peter was thirteen years old , his grandpa
took him to one of their regular walks in the near
forest. They found a nice place to sit on a small
hill overlooking the beautiful forested valley

below.
Grandpa told his grandson ,that this small hill overlooking the valley it was his own grandfather's   favorite spot and they had many visits there when he was a child.

He then told peter that when he was thirteen years old and they were sitting in the exact same spot, his grandfather told him a story about an old man and the advice that man gave his son when he was growing up.

Peter was curious about that man and   he wanted
to know all about that old man to his son.
His grandfather looked at the   spreading vast
green   valley below, took a deep breath and then
looked at young Peter and told him the story
exactly as his own grandfather told him many
years before.

That old man had a   son   and the advice to his son

was this:

Son life is unpredictable and nobody knows what

it will happen next and sometimes the decision we make to day will haunt us years later. Now I made my fair share of some bad choices in my life and I paid for it and I made some good choices in my life and I was rewarded for it. I want you to be careful with your own choices in life , hoping that you will make the right decisions for you. He went on to say that the old man told his son that he was free to do anything he wants to do in life, but anything you decide to do, go and ask the advise of the number one in that field first and then make your own decision. You observe first

and then decide.

If you want to smoke, no problem, but go and talk to the number one smoker first, to see how his life turn out to be with that smoking decision he made.

if you want to gamble, go and see the number one
gambler and see how his life turn out to be with
that gambling decision he made.

 if you want to do any illicit drugs, no problem, but
first go and see the number one drug user and see
how his life turned out to be with using illicit

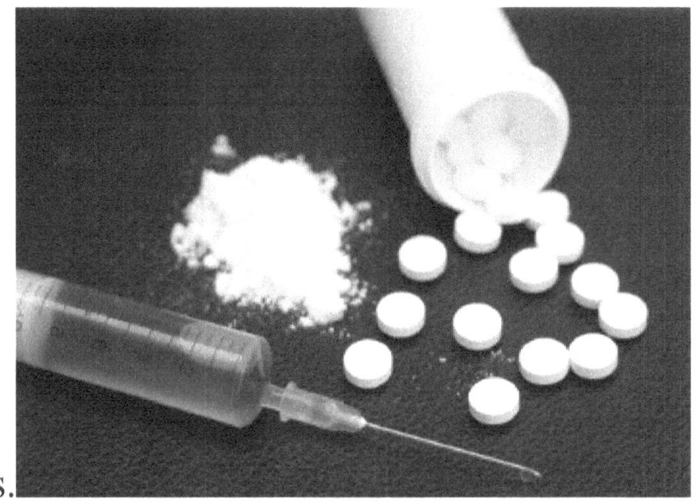

drugs.

If you want to drink alcohol, no problem , but first
go and visit the number one chief drinker in town
and see how his life turn out to be with his

drinking decision.

 The son of the old man promised his father that he
will take his advice before deciding what he was
going to do and report back to him about his
decisions in a few months time.

As promised, the son of that old man ,went to see the chief smoker first and get his opinion about smoking .
He found him all hooked up in a hospital with a respirator having problems to breath suffering from a severe cancer of his lungs.

He asked one of the nurses there, if smoking can do such severe damage to the lungs.

The nurse told him that smoking can turn a healthy lung looking like an old chimney black and charred and useless for breathing and to demonstrate her point, she showed him the x-rays' of the chief smoker. He was so upset from looking at those x-rays and the condition of the chief smoker ,that he vowed never to smoke any kind of smoke. He even vowed to avoid any places that other people were smoking so that he did not have to breath the polluted air from the smoke in that place.

The son of the old man,   then went to see the
chief gambler and get his expert opinion on
gambling. He found the chief gambler living in a
old   tent   near the public beach.

He asked him what happened to all his winnings
from his gambling and ended up living in a tent.
The gambler told him that gambling is very good
but only when you win and very bad when you
loose, and as you can see I lost everything and I
live in this old tent. If gambling was a profitable
job, nobody will want to work, and easy comes
easy goes and when it goes, you end up with
nothing. Take my advice young man and get a real
job with benefits. The son of the old man was very
disappointed with the advice of the gambler, as he
was hoping that gambling will make him rich
someday. However Seeing how the chief

gambler ended up with his gambling decision, he decided never to gamble. The fear of loosing his hard earned money and end up like the chief gambler was a big risk to take.

 In the next few days the son of the old man went to town looking to meet the chief drinker of the town. After many days of searching to find the chief drinker of the town , somebody pointed out to him the chief drinker.

The chief drinker was dressed in dirty old clothes leaning on old bench and holding an almost empty bottle of cheap wine. From time to time the chief drinker, was yelling out loud insults to the passers-by. The son of the old man was afraid to approach or talk to the drunk man. He stayed far away from the chief drinker trying to understand how he

ended up in such a miserable condition. He asked a
passer-by if he knew the drunk man and how he
ended up in such a deplorable condition. The man
told him that he new very well that drunk man, and
that he used to have a business and he had a
family, a wife and a son, but after he started
drinking , he lost his business and his wife
divorced him and took their son and moved to
another town. You see young man, alcohol can
really mess up the lives of people by destroying
their brains and their judgment. It can even kill
you before your time is up.
The son of the old man walked away disheartened
with what he heard from the other man and the
deplorable condition of the drunk man he had
witnessed. He whispered to himself: that's no way
to live man, that's no way to waste your life!

The son of the old man, He then went to see the

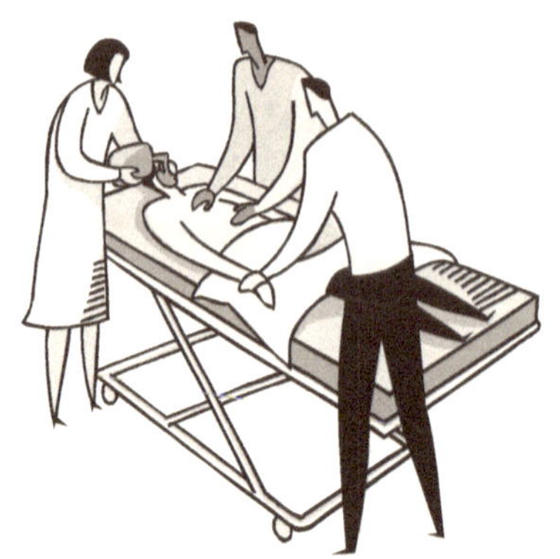

chief drug user.   He had
a hard time locating the chief drug user , but
finally He found him dead from an overdose in
the hospital morgue. The chief drug user was
only 31 years old and he died from a cocktail of
drugs. The man at the morgue did not let him see
the dead man, but he told him that he often sees
many drug users ending up dead in the morgue ,
and their average age is a lot younger than the
chief drug user. Once a person is hooked on drugs
is very hard to escape from the drug addiction and
their health sooner or later will suffer even if they
manage to quit the drug addiction.
The man at the morgue finished by saying: I have
seen so many young persons wasting their young
life with drugs, so Young man, if you want my
honest opinion about drugs, stay away from this
deadly addiction.
The son of the old man walked away, thinking
that he liked his life and in no way he was going

to waste his life with the deadly drugs and die young.

The son of the old man went home and told his father that he just finished visiting the experts of smoking, the gambling, the drinking and the drug users. He went on to tell his father that from what he saw how those people were wasting their lives with smoking, drinking, gambling and drugs use ,that he made up his mind never to do any of those things.
The old man smiled and told his son that he made a wise decision. The son of the old man thank him for helping him to make the right decision. The son of the old man kept his promise to his father and he never smoke, gamble, use drugs or drinking. He became a business man and had a nice family of his own with five kids.

Peter's grandpa finished by saying that was the end of the old man's story and the advise he gave to his son, but the point of the old man's advise is that everyone makes his or her own choices in life and they have to live with the consequences of their actions. And it does pay to investigate before making any choice in life.

Peter looked at his grandpa and told him that was a nice story, although he did not like the gruesome details and the suffering of those people with their addictions. He then asked him if that story had any influence on his own life after hearing it from his own grandpa so many years before. He told peter , yes that's why I never smoke, drink, gamble and never touched any drugs . By making the right choices in my life,, had a great influence in my health and my wallet and I thank grandpa for sharing that story and helping me make the right decisions.

It was getting late in the afternoon so peter and his grandpa   went home .
Peter finished public school with good marks and went to high school.
During the high school years some of his classmates were smoking others were drinking and some of them were even experimenting with drugs. Peter was always remembering the story of the old man and the advice to his son , and he never touched any of that stuff. He always visited his grandfather and many times he thanked him for the story of that old man.
After high school Peter went to the university and became a professor in psychology and many times he shared the story of the old man and the advice to his son with his students, hoping that his

students will make the right choices for their lives.
Peter married his high school sweetheart and they
had a family of their own with two beautiful kids a
boy and a girl.
Peter's parents now retired, are very proud of
peter and his family and they often are
babysitting for their grandkids.

Over the years Peter kept close contact with his
friend Roy who became a mathematician and he
was teaching in the local university. He was also
married and had a family with three kids.
They often had dinners and entertainment with
their families and their kids were friends.
They often talked about their classmates and
their achievements in life . Some of them were
successful in life and others   were struggling
with problems. One of their classmates had an
accident after drinking and driving and ended up in
a wheelchair. Another one died from drug
overdose , and others had problem with drugs,
smoking and gambling addictions. Their choices
in life affected the quality of their lives.
Peter's grandpa died at the ripe age of 97 and he
was in relatively good health up to the time of his
death . His grandmother Annette died six months
later at the age of 95. They were buried side by side
in the local cemetery. Peter often visits his
grandparents grave and every time he thanks

grandpa for telling him the story of the old man and the advice he gave to his son about choices in in life. That story ,helped   Peter to make the right choices in his life, avoiding smoking, drinking gambling and drugs.

Life keeps going, some people come and some people go in the endless cycle of life and they all have to live with the consequences of their choices. Peter was a lucky man he made the right choices and had a good life. Others are not so lucky with their choices and they pay for their bad choices in life.

Here are some poems I wrote about choices in life
.

I wrote the poem "what is your vice" , because almost everyone has a vice of some sort. Some vices are insignificant and does not affect the peoples lives , but other vices are strong addictions with debilitating effects of those affected.

What is your vice

  people have a vice
Some have a small vice
they manage without any advice
 others have a huge vice
 they need a huge advice

Tell me what's your vice
I tell you who is paying the price
If smoking is your vice
Your lungs will pay the price
If drinking is your vice
Your brain will pay the price

Tell me what's your vice
I tell you who is paying the price
If gambling is your vice
 your pocket will pay the price
If drugs is your vice
Your health will pay the price
get advice before you get this vice

Tell me what's your vice
I tell you who is paying the price
If short skirts is your vice
Your pocket will pay the price

Whatever is your vice?
Take my advice , get rid of that vice
Life is a joy without a vice
Live your life without a vice

I wrote the poem "Don't drink and
drive "   when I watched on television
the accident of a drunk man with
another car driven by a sober
grandfather who was taking his grand
kids to school. The drunk driver
survived the accident, but the
grandfather and his kids were all
killed instantly. The drunk driver
eventually went to jail, but   it had
devastated results in the family that
lost two innocent kids and their
grandfather.

DON'T DRINK AND DRIVE
© 2019 by S.ELIA

if you want to stay alive
don't drink and drive
stay alive, stay alive
never ever drink and drive

if you have to drink
leave the driving to others
so that you and others arrive home
alive
stay alive, stay alive
never ever drink and drive

its never fair (for you) to drink and
drive
and others pay the price
even end up in ice
never ever drink and drive
let others do the drive

its never cool
  to drink and drive
it makes you look like a fool
  you can end up in a bloody pool
stay alive, stay alive
never ever drink and drive

if you drink for fun
your brain will hit the fan
spinning around, and around
until you hit the ground
  if you get up and drive
You'll end up in the ground
stay alive, stay alive
never ever drink and drive

if you drink to forget

think what you'll get
a spinning head,
that can get you and others dead
stay alive, stay alive
never ever drink and drive

just remember this
your mother wants you alive
your kids need you alive
everyone else wants to stay alive
please don't drink and drive
stay alive, stay alive
never ever   drink and drive

I wrote the " Boy if you are smart
after reading in the newspaper that a
teenage boy took the family car, got
drunk   and had an accident resulting
in the death of his passenger friend .
The drunk teenage was severely injured
but survived.

Boy if you are smart
© 2019 by S.ELIA

Boy if you are smart
 make a good start
 always play it safe
never get involved in anything
 Illegal, or unsafe

 Take care of your body and mind
 Make yourself one of a kind
 Treat others as you want to be treated
Respect yourself and others,
 Avoid anything bad for your body or mind

Boy if you are smart
You will choose good friends
Friends can make or break you
Good friends make your life a bliss
Bad friends make your life an abyss

Boy if you're smart
You will never make a bad start
Smoking any type of smoke
 ruins your health and leaves you broke
Drinking alcohol ruins   body and mind
makes you sick out of your mind

Boy if you are smart
You never touch any a drug
 That mess up your brain
 Causing you, and others pain
Boy be smart ,Make the right choice ,
live your life with no vice!

I wrote the poem " Girl if your smart", after
watching about girls going partying in night
clubs, getting drunk and sexually abused while

they were drunk. Some of those sexual assaults
ended up in the courts . Some of the accused men
were acquitted and some of them were convicted
and the girls had a lesson in life that will never
forget, that bad choices have consequences.

Girl if you are smart
.(c) 2019   by S.ELIA

Girl if you are smart,
You will never make a bad start
Any kind of smoke is a bad start
Alcohol or drugs is the worse start

Smoking will scar your lungs
 Harm your health, fade your beauty
Will put you off duty
Alcohol and drugs will mess up your brain
Will cause you and others a lot of pain

If you are drinking for fun
 your brain will hit the fan
Spinning around and around
You will never know who is around
 for another round

Girl It was never meant a girls night out
 to drink until you pass out
Strangers will abuse you

They pay no cent
They won't ask for your consent

Girl have pride,
you are not a piece of meat for anyone to use
 have self respect , expect respect
never let yourself open to abuse

Girl if you are smart
 never make a bad start
 never smoke any type of smoke
never drink until you are broke
You will never take any drug
 that can put you in a bag

Girl if you are smart
you make a good start
take healthy staff
 to make you healthy, beautiful and smart
 never touch any bad staff

Girl if you are smart,
You will never make a bad start
you follow good advice ,
 avoid any vice
 have a healthy life
have a good man in your life.

Book description

This book is about the choices people make in life.
This book is written with the hope that people will choose to make better choices for their lives.
Ultimately people are responsible for the choices they make in life and the consequences of those choices
It is my hope that people who read this book will help them make the right choices for their lives, especially if they are still young.
People should always weigh the pros

and cons of any choice they make in
life.
People should learn from the good
choices other people make.
People should also learn from the
bad choices of others and try to
avoid the bad choices.

In this book you will also find some
poems I wrote about the vices
afflicting society, especially the
young people.